Zensho W.Kopp

Living
in inner
fullness

We have the tendency of confusing happiness with pleasure, without realising that pleasure is just an illusion – a shadow of happiness.

True happiness can only be found in the Ever-lasting; only in that which is independent of space and time.

Spiritual desire is a calling of the Eternal; a longing from within the depths of the heart.

That which exists concealed at our innermost depths lies in silence and tranquillity, and in this peace of the depths of divine origin there flows the eternal, inexhaustible original source of all existence.

In Zen it is never a question of suppressing thinking but rather of surpassing thinking.

If you really want to enter into the realm of Enlightenment it is absolutely necessary that you make your mind clear so that it is empty like the void.

Simply leave the mind in its inherent true nature.

The ultimate mystery of all being is experienced in the absoluteness of the self within ourselves as an "I am", which we perceive in the depths of our own being.

In the light of pure consciousness shines the divine Being, the eternal "I am". It is everything in all things, and whoever recognises it experiences himself and the entire creation as this "I am".

In every form of daily life the fundamental and omnipresent reality of Divine Being manifests itself – you need only immerse yourself in it.

Simply make your mind free of everything, whatever it may be. Thus your mind will be unattached, even when it moves within the realm of life and death.

Stop seeking happiness in external things and turn your mind inwards.

Your true being is a boundless ocean of bliss.

The radiating light of divine being is constantly present. It is covered only by the dark clouds of discriminating thought.

True meditation must encompass each moment in life.

Return again and again to pure self-awareness and you will make progress on the spiritual path.

Do not push your spiritual practice into the future, for you do not know if tomorrow you will still be alive.

If you do not make efforts in this life to reach liberation, which life are you going to wait for?

Your true being is completely pure and radiating – just like the bright moon in the night sky.

The "I" is unreal and temporal like a fleeting wave on the surface of the ocean of consciousness.

Recognise that you are pure consciousness, beyond birth and death.

By becoming empty of everything that is not God, we will become filled with the fullness of divine being.

Wherever a person is prepared to abandon himself out of love of the Divine, in complete relinquishment of his self, he will be granted the ascent of the inner light.

The mirror-like awareness of the mind is the pillar of true Zen meditation. Turn your consciousness into a mirror which reflects everything that happens – without taking heed of it.

During meditation, leave the mind in its natural state. All correcting by means of intervention is wrong and only leads to mental exhaustion.

In the silence of the mind you return to your original nature.

The mystery of the immortality of your true being can only be found in the present moment of Now.

Only when you become free from your expectations of wanting to achieve some-thing, will you be on the true path of Zen.

A single moment of the absolute presence of pure consciousness and you are in the timeless eternity of Now.

Do not seek reality externally, for your own mind is Buddha.

If you wish to experience reality then look into your own being, for this being is reality itself.

Your true essence is the all-embracing wholeness of being.

Everything is the One Reality. Everything is the revelation of the truth. There is nothing that exists which is not a manifestation of reality.

You are right in the midst of the Bodhiman-dala – in the great mandala of the multidi-mensional experience of the all-embracing wholeness of being, which pervades the entire universe.

Paradise can be nowhere else than right there where you are "now-here". You do not expe-rience reality right there where you currently are, although it is directly before you, because you are not able to recognise it.

The omnipresence of the One Mind pervades the entire universe. All change and transformation is the continuous self-evolvement and self-transformation of this universal mind.

When you awaken to the reality of your true being, you recognise that everything is the One Mind, beside which nothing else exists. Everything is the One and the One is everything.

Your birth is not the beginning of your life. Your true being precedes your birth, which means that you are life itself. And if your true being is already there before your birth, it will also be there after your death.

Your true being can never be the past and it can never be the future. For these are just clouds which pass by over the clear light of the mind and are unreal.

What you are seeking is your true divine self, beyond space and time, birth and death. It is your own reality. You have never lost it, it is always present.

Detach yourself from your old concepts and from all attachment. Shatter all your limitations. If you follow this, you are truly on the path to Enlightenment.

Only when you have achieved relinquishment by forgetting yourself and all things will peace and the fullness of Divine Being be bestowed on you in the state of mind of inner detachment.

As long as a person only strives towards Enlightenment for himself, he will never gain Enlightenment. For in order to break through to this liberating awakening, a profound insight into the consubstantiality of all beings is required. This requires the spiritual seeker to adopt an intrinsic spiritual attitude which opens itself without any limitation to life in its universality.

We are light of light, which shines in the darkness as our true self. Yet where will you search for the reality of your true being – which you yourself are – except within your-self? Only in a radical self-sacrifice to the abyss of the divine darkness does the radia-ting light appear, which reveals itself as the fullness of the Great Life.

Whoever, out of love of the Eternal, lets go of his small temporal life, simultaneously opens himself to the Great Life beyond space and time, which is waiting for him. Ultimately, this means nothing less than completely letting go, without the least reassurance.

In this inner voidness we are in accordance with the Beatitude spoken by Jesus in the Sermon on the Mount, "Blessed are the pure in heart: for they shall see God."

If we do not truly experience the present moment, we miss out on true life, for the reality of our true being only reveals itself in Here and Now.

When you immerse yourself in what is Now-Here, the realm of ultimate reality, which was previously concealed to you as the thinker, will reveal itself to you.

Be completely clear in the present moment and you experience the entire essence of being as a wonderful revelation of divine reality.

We can only experience the dimension of the boundless reality of the One Mind in absolute Now. This is the multidimensional experience of the all-embracing wholeness of being.

Crystal-clear awareness is the cheerful, relaxed reflection of the mind in the powerful tranquillity of non-thinking.

When your mind is absolutely resolute and quintessentially clear, you will pervade everything and will abide in great calm and unshakeable peace.

Observe your mind in peaceful tranquillity and cheerfulness. Thus you achieve cheerful, serene reflection of the Mind.

Make your mind wide, open and clear, and let it flow freely, without dwelling on anything. This is how you will melt with the essential and achieve indwelling wisdom.

The boundless enlightened-empty conscious-ness is the original state of the Mind.

Observe your own mind, everywhere and at all times. Through this practice you will realise your original buddha-nature.

During Zen meditation it is essential to maintain undistracted, alert awareness in the silence of non-thinking, without allowing yourself to be torn away by external influen-ces or inner thoughts.

When all thoughts dissolve in the crystal-clear awareness of the mind, pure consciousness reveals itself just as it is.

Through continual awareness of your true being you reach a state of unwavering peace.

When you have achieved enduring, absolute awareness you will recognise that you and the universe of highest reality are not separated.

Samadhi is a mental state of crystal-clear awareness together with the absence of thoughts. This is the original, natural state of being of the mind.

The discriminating mind is just a bundle of thoughts and has no reality of its own. The thought-free, empty mind is the pristine state and is filled with bliss.

He who has completely awakened recognises the entire universe within himself and thus experiences everything as this one Self.

The external world of phenomena only exists in your own mind. It changes constantly but the true Self-Mind remains eternally un-changing.

In order to grasp divine reality in all its entirety, you must clear your mind and immerse yourself in the silence of inner contemplation of your true essence.

When you reach the origin of true essence, the self-mind is boundlessly open, dazzlingly bright and lights up the entire universe.

When the false "I" with its illusory world wanes, the light of divine reality radiates forth in the innermost depths of the heart.

The inner sun of understanding will only rise when, in forgetting yourself and all things, the darkness of night has completely engulfed you.

In experiencing the Great Death, no perception of the existence of all things or the ego remains. You just feel how your mind extends to ten thousand worlds and an endless blaze of light appears.

In the experience of all-embracing love and consubstantiality you perceive that everything is pervaded by divine essence and there is no duality.

When you have achieved peace of the self, the whole world is in order and everything is good, just as it is.

In the silence of the mind the immortal mind arises and you abide in the serene peace of the self.

Only your discriminating conceptual thinking separates you from the experience of the splendour of your intrinsic buddha-nature.

Your life has only as much meaning and depth as you have consciousness. Only in the light of pure consciousness will everything become meaningful and precious.

The shortest way to God is through loving devotion of the heart.

The soul, which yearns for God, can be consoled by nothing other than divine love.

When you experience divine love, your whole life becomes a mystical celebration.

Recognise the present thought in its true nature. Look at it directly. In this way, the stream of thoughts is abruptly broken and as long as you remain undistracted, no new conceptual thinking arises.

When your mind is detached and relaxed, all embroilment in thoughts and feelings stops, so that you need not avoid nor manipulate them.

Experiencing your true self, which is the meaning and purpose of your human birth, is not anything special or elitist but instead, it is true life itself.

Your true self is closer to you than your own heart. It is original, pure consciousness and the basis of all experiences. As the true nature of your mind, it is completely beyond every-thing which the normal consciousness is able to fathom.

No meditation takes place when you cannot let your mind relax within itself. Therefore, leave your mind unoccupied, intentionless and relaxed, and then it will come to rest naturally, all of its own accord.

Leave your mind relaxed and detached. When you attempt to cling to your mind, it reacts with increasing thought activity. Yet if you do not cling to it, to comes to rest and becomes silent and clear.

Your consciousness becomes silent of its own accord when, in presence of mind, you let your mind relax without any goal or object on which to meditation.

Gather your mind inwardly, leave it spacious, without any notions. When you are undistracted, you do not become caught in conceptual thinking.

Since all phenomena do not exist beyond the mind but instead are solely the visible light of the mind, the enchainment to phenomena dissolves as soon as you understand the true nature of the mind.

When the consciousness diverges from its intrinsic nature, the intellect moves within its conditioned patterns of delusion. Therefore, allow your consciousness to open here and now in the experience of your true being.

A normal person turns outwards in order to satisfy his unrest. The spiritual seeker turns to his heart and thus achieves fulfilment.

In utter silence of the mind your heart receives and understands everything.

The reason for our being bound to birth and death is that we do not perceive the true nature of our mind. This ignorance causes all deceptive thoughts to arise, which bind us to the karmic law of cause and effect.

Pure, objectless meditation is when you immerse yourself in the origin of your true essence.

Pure Zen meditation means diving into the boundless mind of the Buddha-nature and thus manifesting the essence of all buddhas.

The original state of the perfection of the mind can only be experienced in the absolute Now of pure awareness, beyond past, present and future.

Through lasting non-distraction and constant, present awareness of mind you shatter all illusions and enter the highest path to Enlightenment.

During the course of many incarnations, a strong habit of self-distraction has arisen in the mind. Therefore it is very important to be undistracted and presently aware, and to maintain this awareness constantly in all the activities of daily life.

Undistracted, present awareness is the key to self-perception in daily life.

When thoughts arise during meditation, practise presence of mind, without viewing the thoughts as erroneous. In this way, the thoughts will become more and more subtle until they cease of their own accord and the experience of peaceful clarity and non-thinking takes place.

When you have returned to your true, original nature, your whole being resides in harmonious unison with the all-embracing wholeness of existence.

Everywhere and constantly, the fullness of divine being reveals itself to you.

Everything is a revelation of divine reality. Everything is filled with the fullness of God.

Neither before nor after exist. There is only Now, and this Now is the reality of divine being.

In Zen, mindfullness is a continuous and object-free awareness of the Self-Mind.

Constantly retain a completely relaxed state of mind and a crystal-clear awareness in all that you do.

Our true self is unborn and unbound, and is not affected by the impermanence of the body with all its mental and physical changes.

The light of truth in the heart will only shine when we have liberated ourselves from the identification with body, mind and world.

The direct Zen way to liberation is when you retain your inner stability and serenity in the midst of the demands of everyday life.

Everything is an all-encompassing whole which contains everything within itself.

Silence your thoughts and immerse yourself in the all-embracing wholeness of being.

When your mind abides nowhere and is completely detached from its clinging to sense impressions and random thoughts, regardless of whether you live in the midst of the hustle and bustle of the world, your mind will be completely empty and in silent peace and one with the Absolute.

Image editing: Reinhard Zanella,
Jörg Zimmermann, Sandro Hölzel
Typesetting/Cover-Design: Jörg Zimmermann
Portrait photograph: Axel Jung
Translation: John Kitching

EAN / ISBN-13
9783751957731

Picture credits can be found in the original German version
of this book, titled "Leben aus der inneren Fülle".

Zensho W. Kopp, born 1938, is considered to be one of the most significant wisdom teachers of the present and teaches a contemporary way to spiritual realisation.

The internationally renowned author of numerous spiritual books and audio CDs instructs a large community of students and directs the Zen Center Tao Chan in Wiesbaden, Germany.

Tao Chan Zentrum e.V. Nonprofit organisation, Wiesbaden, Germany

Public Zen-Evening: Twice a month, the Zen Center Tao Chan organises a Zen-evening, open to all and led by Zen Master Zensho W. Kopp.

Information on the events can be found at:
www.tao-chan.org/ and **www.facebook.com/zensho.w.kopp**
Video talks by Master Zensho can be found here:
www.tao-chan.org/zen-master-zensho/videos.html

Further publications of the author Zen Master Zensho W. Kopp

All books available at: www.tao-chan.org

Modern ZEN-ART
Watercolours and sayings of a Western Zen Master

ISBN 978-3-907246-09-2   DE /EN

Awakening to Your True Self
The Zen way of all-embracing mysticism

ISBN 978-3-751931-82-3

True Life Through Zen
Spiritual self-realisation in daily life

ISBN 978-3-734743-55-9

Lao-tse – Tao Te King
The Book of Tao and Spiritual Force

Transcription by Zen Master Zensho W. Kopp

ISBN 978-3-842328-61-7

Words of the Awakened Mind
Aphorisms of a Western Zen Master

ISBN 978-3-848241-34-7

Enlightened Dimensions of the Divine
Paintings and quotations of a Western Zen Master

ISBN 978-1-4827-9942-2

The Freedoom of Zen
The Zen book that shatters all limits and bounds

ISBN 978-3751937-01-6